P9-BYD-655

Presented to

From

Date

WORD PUBLISHING
Nashville • London • Vancouver • Melbourne

to deserve her love every morning
and Butterfly Kisses at night.
All the precious time
like the wind, the years go by.
Precious butterfly
spread your wings and fly.

She'll change her name today.
She'll make a promise, and I'll give her away.
Standing in the bride room just staring at her,
she asked me what I'm thinking,
and I said, "I'm not sure.
I just feel like I'm losing my baby girl."
Then she leaned over and gave me . . .

Butterfly Kisses, with her momma there
sticking little white flowers all up in her hair.
"Walk me down the aisle Daddy,
it's just about time."
"Does my wedding gown look pretty Daddy?"
"Daddy, don't cry."
With all that I've done wrong,
I must have done something right
to deserve her love every morning,
and Butterfly Kisses . . .

I couldn't ask God for more,
man, this is what love is.
I know I've gotta let her go,

but I'll always remember . . .
every hug in the morning
and Butterfly Kisses . . .

BOB CARLISLE

Reflections from a

Father and His Daughter

in Their Own Words

A journal of

Butterfly

Kisses

BOB CARLISLE
BUTTERFLY KISSES™

Copyright © 1997 Bob Carlisle, Nashville, TN

Published by Word Publishing, a division of Thomas Nelson, Inc.,
Nashville, TN 37214

Compiled and edited by Terri Gibbs.

All rights reserved. No portion of this publication may be reproduced, stored
in a retrieval system or transmitted in any form by any means—electronic,
mechanical, photocopying, recording, or any other—except for brief quotations
in printed reviews, without the prior written permission of the publisher.

The song "Butterfly Kisses" words and music by Bob Carlisle & Randy Thomas.
Copyright © 1996 Diadem Music Publishing and Polygram International
Publishing, Inc. International Copyright Secured. All Rights Reserved.
Used with permission.

The complete poems "Lovely Saturday" and "Not Yours, but You" originally
appeared in *Clouds Are the Dust of His Feet* by Ruth Bell Graham, 1992. The
excerpts here are used with permission. © Ruth Bell Graham.

J. Countryman is a trademark of Word Publishing, a division of Thomas
Nelson, Inc.

A J. Countryman Book

Designed by Koechel Peterson & Associates, Inc.,
Minneapolis, Minnesota

ISBN: 08499-5354-5

Contents

Foreword

$\mathcal{I}$ don't know why it is, but the hurried lives we live these days allow too little time for the truly important things—like talking to each other. As I think back on it, that is the reason I wrote "Butterfly Kisses" for my daughter Brooke. I was struck by the fact that this girl was growing up and would soon be off on her own. The song poured out of me as an expression of my gratitude—that in spite of my shortcomings, this little girl had grown into a wonderful woman and I wanted her to know it.

$\mathcal{I}$ have heard from hundreds of fathers and daughters who have told me their own stories. Each of these stories is unique. Some relate joyous experiences. Some talk with regret about missed opportunities. But all are filled with deep feelings and a desire to relate something specific and vital about the special relationships of fathers and daughters.

$\mathcal{E}$very time I read one of these stories I am reminded how important it is for us as families to take time to write down the experiences of life we share together. That is the purpose for this journal. It's a place for fathers to express in their own words what it feels like to hold a newborn daughter for the first time. It's a place for a daughter to remember her father's praise for homework well-done. It's a place to write down the important things that might not get said otherwise.

$\mathcal{J}$ encourage you, fathers and daughters, to use this journal to record the little incidents that have special meaning for you. When all is come and gone, it is these little things strung together through time that make up our lives. And it is in sharing our lives together that it all becomes apparent.

Bob Carlisle

Butterfly Kisses

There's two things I know for sure.
She was sent here from heaven,
and she's Daddy's little girl.
As I drop to my knees by her bed at night,
she talks to Jesus, and I close my eyes.
And I thank God for all of the joy in my life,
but most of all, for . . .

Butterfly Kisses after bedtime prayer.
Stickin' little white flowers all up in her hair.
"Walk beside the pony Daddy, it's my first ride."
"I know the cake looks funny Daddy,
but I sure tried."
Oh, with all that I've done wrong,
I must have done something right
to deserve a hug every morning
and Butterfly Kisses at night.

Sweet Sixteen today,
she's looking like her momma
a little more every day.
One part woman, the other part girl.
To perfume and makeup,
from ribbons and curls.
Trying her wings out in a great big world.
But I remember . . .

Butterfly Kisses after bedtime prayer.
Stickin' little white flowers all up in her hair.
"You know how much I love you Daddy,
but if you don't mind, I'm only going
to kiss you on the cheek this time."
With all that I've done wrong,
I must have done something right

Butterfly Kisses
from Dad

The ridiculous charm of
making funny faces at a
child is that it makes a
child out of the person
making faces.

TERRY LINDVALL

BABY LOUISE

I'm in love with you, Baby Louise!
With your silken hair,
and your soft blue eyes,
And the dreamy wisdom
that in them lies,
And the faint, sweet smile
you brought from the skies,
—God's sunshine, Baby Louise

M.E.

These were my thoughts
upon seeing you for the first time.

_____

_____

_____

_____

_____

_____

This is what I felt like
when I first held you in my arms.

_____

_____

_____

_____

_____

_____

We have chosen for our daughter the name of MaryAnne's
mother—Andrea. What a thing it is to be introduced to one's
child. I find a new side to my being that even the gentility of
MaryAnne could not produce from my brutal soul.

David Parkin's Diary, January 18, 1909

Timepiece

RICHARD PAUL EVANS

LULLABY

from "The Princess"

Sleep and rest, sleep and rest,
Father will come to thee soon;
Rest, rest, on mother's breast,
Father will come to thee soon;
Father will come to his
> babe in the nest,
Silver sails all out of the west
Under the silver moon:
Sleep, my little one, sleep,
> my pretty one, sleep.

ALFRED TENNYSON

Standing before a cradle a father seems face to face with the attributes of the everlasting Being who has infused His tenderness and love into the babe.

FULTON J. SHEEN

I will never forget the cute things
you said as a little girl. _____

_____

_____

_____

_____

_____

_____

_____

*O*ne of the funniest things
you did when you were small was _____

_____

_____

_____

_____

_____

_____

_____

_____

*M*ay your father and mother be glad; may she who gave you
birth rejoice!

PROVERBS 23:25

There is nothing that moves a loving father's soul quite like his child's cry.

JONI EARECKSON TADA

My child's feelings are hurt. I tell her she's special. My child is injured. I do whatever it takes to make her feel better. My child is afraid. I won't go to sleep until she is secure. . . . Moments of comfort from a parent. As a father, I can tell you they are the sweetest moments in my day. They come naturally. They come willingly. They come joyfully.

MAX LUCADO

The Applause of Heaven

I remember some of the things
that made my little girl cry.

_____

_____

_____

_____

_____

_____

_____

_____

_____

And some of the things
that made her laugh.

_____

_____

_____

_____

_____

_____

_____

_____

_____

_____

My dad, the young preacher John Wood, was tall and slim, with black hair always combed neatly and soft brown eyes with a glint of mischief in them. And, I thought, very handsome! He was gregarious, full of good humor, fond of teasing and practical jokes. . . .

Because Dad chose to have his office at home rather than at the church, I saw more of my father than most children do.

Often I would creep into his home office unbidden, but he was never too busy for me. Invariably he would smile and hold out his arms to receive me. "Girlie—my girlie," he would say.

CATHERINE MARSHALL

The Best of Catherine Marshall

If I had to choose one word
to describe you as a little girl it would be

_____

because _____

_____

_____

These are some of the activities I enjoyed
doing with you as you were growing up.

1. _____

_____

2. _____

_____

3. _____

_____

4. _____

_____

5. _____

_____

Often the deepest relationships can be developed during

the simplest activities.

GARY SMALLEY

The most fun thing we ever did together was

_____

_____

_____

_____

_____

_____

I especially enjoyed it because _____

_____

_____

_____

_____

_____

_____

Play allows us to be eternally young, to be like children
even when we are old and wrinkly.

TERRY LINDVALL

With children who thrive
on simple pleasures,
our work and our entire
society can be renewed.

SARA WENGER SHENK

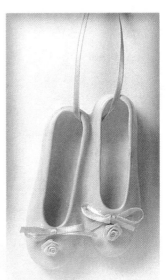

If we savor the good
times in youth, we can
enjoy them again in
old age.

JEANETTE OKE

The interaction in our house is not always gentle and serene. It's just as likely to be rambunctious and rowdy. The pillows of our large family room sofas get thrown a lot during our family gymnastics sessions. We roll on the floor; we wrestle. The girls play "Hop on Pop," which means they sit on my chest and bounce up and down like kangaroos. . . . These are wonderful times we have together, full of the innocence of childhood and the warmth of family togetherness.

The girls love those times. Nanette and I love them too. . . . We love feeling breathless with laughter and love.

THOMAS KINKADE

Simpler Times

I am so proud of your accomplishments as you were growing up. Here are a few that stand out in my mind.

1. _____

_____

_____

2. _____

_____

_____

3. _____

_____

_____

4. _____

_____

_____

5. _____

_____

_____

Men love their children, not because they are promising plants, but because they are theirs.

CHARLES MONTAGU, EARL OF HALIFAX

Home is where one starts from.

T. S. Eliot

I have no recollection of any specific word my father spoke when I was very small, but I have a vivid sense of his comforting and sometimes awesome presence. Daddy was either at home or not at home, and the difference was very great. Sometimes I waited in the vestibule, peeping through the mail slot to see him come home from the office, up the porch steps, always dressed in a dark blue suit, white shirt, and conservative tie, always carrying a briefcase. When he opened the door I hugged his knees.

Elisabeth Elliot

The Shaping of a Christian Family

The color that best describes your personality is

_____

because _____

_____

_____

_____

_____

_____

_____

_____

_____

The little buds, may they be bless'd

In doing as they're taught;

May they in loveliness be dress'd,

And ne'er with frowns be caught.

ANONYMOUS

Simple Wisdom

One of the most special gifts
you ever gave to me was _____

_____

_____

_____

This was special to me because _____

_____

_____

_____

_____

_____

_____

_____

_____

Nothing is dearer to an old father than a daughter. Sons have

spirits of higher pitch, but they are not given to fondness.

EURIPIDES 484–406 B.C.

Love is a happy feeling that stays inside your heart for

the rest of your life.

JOAN WALSH ANGLUND

If I could give you anything
in the world I would give you _____

_____

because _____

_____

_____

_____

_____

_____

_____

_____

One of the greatest gifts we can give to our daughters
is a mirror where they can find love colorfully and
truthfully reflected.

DEBRA EVANS

It is not how many things you provide for your children.
It is what you give them of yourself and the principles of
Scripture that can never be taken away.

CHARLES STANLEY

A very familiar scene in my mind is my dad, sitting in his lawn chair, watching from the sidelines as I competed in tennis matches around the area. Somehow he was always there. It was rare for dads to attend weekday matches, but somehow Dad made it seem natural for a man with a full-time job to show up in Houston or Galveston or some other city to watch as the first set began. . . . Sometimes when things went wrong on the court, I'd lose my temper and stomp around the sidelines or make a face. Then I'd see Daddy sitting over there, giving the look that said, *Keep your cool, keep control of your temper, and keep your chin up,* and I'd take a deep breath and get back into the game.

RUTH RYAN (WIFE OF NOLAN RYAN)
Covering Home

God is at home
in the play of His children.
He loves to hear us laugh.

PETER MARSHALL

I still laugh when I think of the
funniest incident from your teen years.

_____

_____

_____

_____

Your reaction to the incident was _____

_____

_____

_____

A special memory from your teen years
that I will always cherish was the time

_____

_____

_____

_____

I cherish this memory because _____

_____

_____

_____

_____

I simply let my children know by the way I treat them that I am glad they are who they are.

SPENCER JOHNSON, M.D.

"*In* spite of the curly crop, I don't see the 'son Jo' whom I left a year ago," said Mr. March. "I see a young lady who pins her collar straight, laces her boots neatly and neither whistles, talks slang, nor lies on the rug as she used to do. . . . I rather miss my wild girl; but if I get a strong, helpful, tender-hearted woman in her place, I shall feel quite satisfied. . . ."

LOUISA MAY ALCOTT
Little Women

When you were growing up, one of
my proudest moments was when you

_____

_____

_____

_____

_____

I was so proud because

_____

_____

_____

_____

Every day my dad teaches me new things. He tells me what
he did after work that day and says if he had a good day or
not. Then he says that he really loves me.

ANGELA, 9

Take Time to Play Checkers

A father's thoughtfulness or thoughtlessness will be
reproduced in his children.

ELISABETH ELLIOT

Dad's lap always seemed more commodious than Mother's, his arms more firm. For me, those arm's were protection and reassurance, warmth, strength, and nourishment. In some strange way, the love that flowed between us must have been nourishment for him, too.

CATHERINE MARSHALL
The Best of
Catherine Marshall

By viewing our daughters from the Creator's perspective— and relying upon His grace to renew our vision day by day— we can mirror their special qualities back to them as the advocates, protectors, and guardians we are called to be.

DEBRA EVANS

If we could live your childhood years
over again I definitely would _____

_____

_____

_____

_____

_____

_____

I definitely would *not* _____

_____

_____

_____

_____

_____

_____

Our words can promote growth by wrapping others in
a cocoon of love and hope.

GARY SMALLEY AND JOHN TRENT

These were my thoughts . . .

on the day you were baptized (dedicated) _____

_____

_____

_____

_____

on your first day at school _____

_____

_____

_____

_____

when you went away to summer camp _____

_____

_____

_____

_____

_____

My thoughts . . .

when you had your first date _____

_____

_____

_____

_____

when you were learning how to drive _____

_____

_____

_____

_____

on the day you graduated _____

_____

_____

_____

_____

_____

My thoughts . . .

when you became engaged

on the day you were married

when you became a mother

I stood outside Jenna's room holding the velveteen case in my hands. My throat was dry as I slid the box into my trouser pocket and knocked gently on the door. A soft voice answered.

"Come in."

I stepped into the room. Jenna sat on her bed writing in her diary. A bridal gown, sheathed in a transparent garment bag, hung from the closet door above a new pair of boxed white satin pumps.

"Hi, sweetheart." . . .

I took my girl in my arms and held her tightly to my chest. My heart, bathed in fond memory, ached in the sweet pain of separation. This is what it meant to be a father—had always meant. To know that one day I would turn around and my little girl would be gone.

RICHARD PAUL EVANS

Timepiece

When our first little girl
was learning to walk,
she would stand on my
husband's feet and he
would waltz with her. Is
this something intuitive?
When I was a small child
I stood on my father's
feet while he danced, too.

MADELEINE L'ENGLE

No one can make a child
love anything, from
spinach to sparrows to
Scripture, but the
parents' love for things
exerts a powerful thrust
in that direction (and I for
one learned to love all of
the above).

ELISABETH ELLIOT

The one word that would describe
your personality as a young lady is _____

_____

because _____

_____

_____

_____

_____

_____

_____

_____

My father always reminded me that there were greater

achievements ahead. His message was that I was not to

stop growing, not to stop stretching.

JENNY WALTON

These are some of the things I especially
appreciate about your gifts and talents:

_____

_____

_____

_____

The way you have developed those gifts
and talents makes me proud because

_____

_____

_____

_____

Fathers are wonderful to have around because their

most important job is to love you.

KRISTIN, 10

Take Time to Play Checkers

A child is fed with milk and praise.

MARY LAMB

There is one thing I have always
wished we could do together. _____

_____

_____

_____

_____

I wish we could do this because _____

_____

_____

_____

_____

LOVELY SATURDAY

There is no one left to walk with now

No small, warm hand within my own

And woods are less enchanting

When explored alone.

RUTH BELL GRAHAM

Clouds Are the Dust of His Feet

You build a successful life one day at a time.

LOU HOLTZ

These are the things you have
going for you as you face the future. _____

_____

_____

_____

_____

_____

As your father I pledge to _____

_____

_____

_____

_____

_____

Happy is he that is happy in his children.

THOMAS FULLER

I liked the way my father had of making people laugh,
and I felt important belonging to him.

INA HUGHS

Sitting there watching you last night made it crystal clear right before my eyes that I was losing my little girl and in her place a very precious woman (and I hope lifelong friend) was emerging. I realized like I never had before the wonderful little changes that are taking place in what you talk about and what you laugh at. I don't know why it should come as sort of a surprise to me, Kelly, but you're truly growing up and I'm loving it 'cause I love you.

JOSH MCDOWELL
Love, Dad

All thy children shall be taught of the LORD; and great shall be the peace of thy children.

ISAIAH 54:13

My daughter Vanessa once was given a helium-filled balloon at Sunday School. It was bright blue, and to a two-year-old it must have seemed almost alive as it danced and floated on the end of a string. She was intrigued by her new toy, and she ran through the halls of the church that day pulling it along behind her, watching it bob brightly in the air above her head.

But the inevitable happened. The balloon finally bumped into the sharp edge of a metal railing and popped. With a single, loud "bang," it burst and fell to her feet. She looked down and saw at the end of the string not a marvelous, bouncing, nearly-alive balloon, but a forlorn wad of wet blue rubber. The sudden transformation seemed to startle her, but only briefly. She paused for only a second, then happily picked up the shredded rubber, marched cheerfully to where I was standing, and thrust it up at me.

"Here, Daddy," she chirped confidently, "fix it!"

CHARLES PAUL CONN

FatherCare

I enjoyed the little "rituals" and
family traditions we shared such as

_____

_____

_____

_____

Some of our rituals and family traditions that
I hope you will pass on to your children include

_____

_____

_____

_____

_____

The caterpillar is probably not on anyone's list of the world's

"ten most beautiful creatures." Yet a caterpillar can potentially

be transformed into a gorgeous butterfly.

GARY SMALLEY AND JOHN TRENT

Then one day you floated down the stairs in crinoline and lace,

a butterfly at last. What happened to gangly legs, to picture

books and climbing trees?

DONNA GREEN

There is nothing quite so deeply satisfying as the solidarity of a family united across the generations and miles by a common faith and history.

SARA WENGER SHENK

The "father-involved" family is a fragile cultural achievement and cannot be taken for granted.

JOHN MILLER

Remember, the key to happiness is _____

_____

_____

_____

_____

_____

_____

_____

_____

_____

_____

_____

The gift of life unwraps itself through time; all we need to do
is sit back and enjoy its contents.

SOUL SEARCHING

Our happiness is greatest when we contribute most to the
happiness of others.

HARRIET SHEPARD

My greatest desire for you is

_____

_____

_____

_____

_____

_____

The best thing to spend on your children is time.

ANONYMOUS

There is one question I just have to ask you.

_____

_____

_____

_____

_____

The simple truth is that fathers are irreplaceable in shaping
the competence and character of their children.

DAVID BLANKENHORN

My security was assured in many ways as a child. Every night I would go to the door of my room in my nightie and call out, "Papa, I'm ready for bed." He would come to my room and pray with me before I went to sleep. I can remember that he always took time with us and he would tuck the blankets around my shoulders very carefully, with his own characteristic precision. Then he would put his hand gently on my face and say, "Sleep well, Corrie . . . I love you."

. . . Many years later in a concentration camp in Germany, I sometimes remembered the feeling of my father's hand on my face.

CORRIE TEN BOOM
In My Father's House

One thing I hope you will
always remember me for is _____

_____

_____

_____

_____

_____

_____

_____

The righteous man walks in his integrity;

His children are blessed after him.

PROVERBS 20:7

Before I got married I had six theories on children;

now I have six children and no theories.

JOHN WILMOT

There is one thing
I have always wanted to tell you. _____

_____

_____

_____

_____

My chest swells with pride and I smile
every time I think of these nice things
that others have said about you. _____

_____

_____

_____

_____

_____

My father often did not let us in on what seemed to me his
deepest thoughts. Men of his generation didn't, I suppose.
What he did give us was his sense of values, by the way he
acted and the things he believed in.

JENNY WALTON

Let me tell you how proud I am of the way you overcame these difficulties and challenges when you were growing up. ___

_____

_____

_____

_____

_____

_____

_____

_____

Never grow a wishbone, daughter,

where your backbone ought to be.

CLEMENTINE PADDLEFORD

Give a little love to a child, and you get a great deal back.

JOHN RUSKIN

Children need love, especially when they don't deserve it.

HAROLD HULBERT

My own father's boast was that he'd washed dishes for my mother the night they met and been doing it every night for forty years. I also cherish happy memories of his bathing his little flock, then with one on each arm of his squeaky rocker and one on his lap, singing us all to sleep.

My mother was not a dominating woman, and she practiced no career. My father worked long and hard at very masculine labor. He did these things for the selfsame reason that thousands of good men do them still: Because he loved his wife and children. And these tasks were the most enjoyable way he knew of to express that love.

MARJORIE HOLMES
Lord, Let Me Love

My dad has always been
a source of encouragement
and emotional support for
me. He's my hero. He's my
friend. And he's always
been in love with my mom.

SHELLY WILLIAMSON

My dad should learn
to cook some food.
If my mom's not home,
my dad just has a big
bowl of ice cream and
some cookies.

HEATHER, 12
*Take Time
to Play Checkers*

These are some of my
special thoughts about your mother.
_____

_____

_____

_____

_____

_____

_____

_____

These are some of the things
I love best about her.
_____

_____

_____

_____

_____

_____

_____

_____

_____

NOT YOURS, BUT YOU

It isn't your gold or silver,

your talents great or small,

your voice, or your gift of drawing,

or the crowd you go with at all; . . .

no, it isn't the things you have, dear,

or the things you like to do,

the Master is searching deeper . . .

He seeks not yours, but you.

RUTH BELL GRAHAM
Clouds Are the Dust of His Feet

A daughter gets from her mother all the mothering stuff. But she gets from her father how she feels about her own worth.

SHERRY ORTLUND

Some books I would encourage you to read are

_____

_____

_____

_____

_____

_____

It has been amazing to watch your life develop.
Some of the wonderful things that make you
one-of-a-kind are _____

_____

_____

_____

_____

_____

_____

_____

This is a Scripture verse I have chosen for you.

Jesus introduced a dizzyingly wonderful new reality:
women as they were meant to be, whole, vigorous, bold,
and filled with joy.

SARA WENGER SHENK

In spite of all the wonderful memories
we share, there are still some things
I wish we had done together . . .

when you were a little girl _____

_____

_____

_____

_____

_____

when you were a teenager _____

_____

_____

_____

_____

_____

Men love grand, abstract, universal theories. Women are
more attached to the details of experience.

PAUL TOURNIER

What I most admire about you . . .

as a little girl _____

_____

_____

as a teenager _____

_____

_____

as a young woman _____

_____

_____

in your career _____

_____

_____

as a wife _____

_____

_____

as a mother _____

_____

_____

One experience from my childhood
that taught me an incredible lesson was _____

_____

_____

_____

_____

_____

_____

_____

_____

Speak gently—it is better far

To rule by love than fear;

Speak gently,—let not harsh words mar

The good we might do here.

ANONYMOUS

Simple Wisdom

The measure of a life, after all, is not its duration
but its donation.

CORRIE TEN BOOM

Here are four tried-and-true principles
I have learned in life.

1. _____

_____

_____

2. _____

_____

_____

3. _____

_____

_____

4. _____

_____

_____

"There's nothing the child can't do. Why, she wanted a pair
of blue boots for Sallie's party, so she just painted her soiled
white ones the loveliest shade of sky-blue you ever saw, and
they looked exactly like satin."

LOUISA MAY ALCOTT
Good Wives

There are still some things
I am looking forward to as your dad.

_____

_____

_____

_____

_____

_____

_____

_____

_____

_____

_____

Dads have no problem bonding with their daughters. A son is
a potential rival (so the psychologists say), but a daughter is his
baby princess and that's that.

RAY ORTLUND

When parents receive a child from the hand of God they
receive a life to be shaped and molded.

ELISABETH ELLIOT

Here are five reasons why
I'm so glad you are my daughter:

1. _____

_____

2. _____

_____

3. _____

_____

4. _____

_____

5. _____

_____

Fathers are as important to daughters as mothers are. Our daughters need us to affirm their mastery and to affirm their femininity. They need to know that the first man in their life is head over heels in love with them.

SAMUEL OSHERSON, PH.D.

A blessing for you from your dad: _____

_____

_____

_____

_____

_____

_____

_____

_____

_____

_____

_____

_____

_____

_____

_____

_____

The father is the priest in the home. This means standing
in the presence of God for others.

ELISABETH ELLIOT

A happy family is but
an earlier heaven.

JOHN BOWRING

Photos

Photos

A little nonsense, now
and then, is relished
by the wisest one.

ANONYMOUS

Hugs from
Daddy's Little Girl

Everywhere,

we learn only from those

whom we love.

JOHANN WOLFGANG VON GOETHE

Dear Dad,

You know how I feel

You listen to how I think

You understand . . .

You're

my

friend.

SUSAN POLIS SCHUTZ

Your pet name for me has always been _____

_____

_____

My earliest memory of you is _____

_____

_____

_____

_____

_____

_____

_____

_____

When Daddy came to tuck me in, he would sit on the bed, and
I would often kneel, reaching up to put my hands on his knees.
With his huge hands on mine he prayed for me.

ELISABETH ELLIOT

To the child a favorite teddy bear is not just a thing,
but a person.

PAUL TOURNIER

When we forget the obvious, the little joys, the meals together, the birthday celebrations, the weeping together in time of pain, the wonder of the sunset or the daffodil peeping through the snow, we become less human.

MADELEINE L'ENGLE

Daddy was the master of spur-of-the-moment parties on a shoestring: a Dairy Queen after church, a roadside picnic breakfast. . . . It was Daddy who gave me my very own garden spot and gave me full rein to plant anything I wanted to.

GLORIA GAITHER

When I was little, one thing
you always did to dry my tears was to _____

_____

_____

_____

_____

You were my "hero" the time you _____

_____

_____

_____

_____

because _____

_____

_____

_____

Always remember to forget the things that made you sad.

But never forget to remember the things that made you glad.

ELBERT HUBBARD

When I was a little girl,
my favorite outing with you was the time we

_____

_____

_____

_____

_____

_____

It was special to me because _____

_____

_____

_____

_____

_____

_____

My father is funny and fun to be around.

BROOKE CARLISLE
(DAUGHTER OF BOB CARLISLE)

When I think of the word *dad*
these words come to my mind. _____

_____

_____

_____

_____

When I used to brag about you
to my friends, I would say _____

_____

_____

_____

_____

When I brag about you now I say _____

_____

_____

_____

_____

*Be glad of life because it gives you the chance to love and to
work and to play and to look up at the stars.*

HENRY VAN DYKE

Had he lived, yesterday would have been Daddy's seventy-sixth birthday. Sometimes I still miss him like he's still here, only gone somewhere, and I find myself waiting for a chance to go home or for him to come home. When things are confused and complicated for me, I think of him as though having home the same would make everything else in the world normal again.

GLORIA GAITHER
We Have This Moment

I can do one of two things. I can be president of the United States or I can control Alice. I cannot possibly do both.

THEODORE ROOSEVELT

Here are three things about you,
Dad, that I would never change:

1. _____

_____

2. _____

_____

3. _____

_____

Here are three things I would change if I could:

1. _____

_____

2. _____

_____

3. _____

_____

I have no greater joy than to hear that my children

walk in truth.

3 JOHN 1:4

The web of our life is of a mingled yarn, good and ill together.

WILLIAM SHAKESPEARE

The most unforgettable gift
you ever gave to me was _____

_____

_____

_____

_____

_____

It was so special because _____

_____

_____

_____

_____

_____

Goodness is the only investment that never fails.

HENRY DAVID THOREAU

*I appreciate the ways you always
let me know you love me.* _____

_____

_____

_____

_____

_____

_____

_____

_____

_____

_____

_____

Daddy affirms my femininity. He compliments me on how
I look; he treats me gently. The guys, he pals with—but me,
he treats as a little fragile.

MARGIE ORTLUND

One thing you always said that has
made a strong impression on my life is _____

_____

_____

_____

_____

_____

These are some of the invaluable lessons
I have learned just by watching your life:

1. _____

_____

_____

2. _____

_____

_____

3. _____

_____

_____

Nothing is so potent as the silent influence of a good example.

JAMES KENT

Today is a promise you
make to yourself.

PEARCE LANE

My father's commitment and faithfulness
to serve God has cost him in many ways,
including limited time with family and, in more
recent years, his health. But by his example,
I knew God was great and Jesus was Lord.

ANNE GRAHAM LOTZ
(DAUGHTER OF BILLY GRAHAM)

One of my fondest memories
of you from my teen years is _____

_____

_____

_____

_____

_____

_____

𝒥 cherish this memory because _____

_____

_____

_____

_____

_____

_____

Prayer is the mortar that holds our house together.

St. Teresa

One of the most fun times we had
together when I was a teenager was _____

_____

_____

_____

_____

This was especially fun because _____

_____

_____

_____

_____

Although Dad is very busy traveling about 100,000 miles
every year, he makes time for me. For the last three years
he has even found time to be my softball coach. He shows his
love by spending time with me. My dad will leave a heritage of
the love and care he shared with me.

I believe I have the best earthly father that my Heavenly Father
would want me to have.

HOLLY BURT

One thing I would still like for us
to do together some day is _____

_____

_____

_____

_____

_____

_____

J hope we can do this because_____

_____

_____

_____

_____

_____

The great man is he who does not lose his child's heart.

MENCIUS

These are some of the valuable
contributions you have made to my life.

1. _____

_____

_____

2. _____

_____

_____

3. _____

_____

_____

4. _____

_____

_____

Women, precisely because they have a keener sense of the person than men have, also need, more than men do, to feel that they are recognized as persons.

PAUL TOURNIER

Dear Dad,

There so many things that I love about you and that I want to thank you for, but there is one thing that I have never told you.

Dad, you are a haven to me. You have this incredible power to make me feel protected and loved no matter what other things are going on in my life. To spend time with you, to talk to you—just to hear your voice on the other end of a phone call puts me at rest. When you tell me everything will be all right, I believe you.

I so clearly remember a time soon after I learned to drive. I was following you back to our house from somewhere we had been because I didn't know the way home. When we were about a mile from our house I was, of course, in very familiar territory. At this point we were separated when I had to stop at a red light that you had already passed through. I wasn't worried though because I knew the way home. But as I looked up ahead I saw you pull off the road to wait for me so that I could continue to follow you home. I smiled to myself as I sat at the light knowing in just that little gesture how much you cared for me. I remember thinking, *I will never forget this moment.*

I love you Dad,

SARAH ZACHARIAS
(DAUGHTER OF RAVI ZACHARIAS)

If I had to select one word to describe
your personality Dad it would be _____

_____

because _____

_____

_____

_____

One of the things I love most about you is _____

_____

because _____

_____

_____

_____

_____

If you have a tender message,

Or a loving word to say,

Do not wait till you forget it,

But whisper it today.

FRANK HERBERT SWEET

Dad, here is a list of some of
your outstanding character traits:

_____

_____

_____

_____

_____

_____

_____

_____

_____

_____

_____

My father was a minister from 1900 to 1940. During those
forty years, his total income was $49,000—and there were
seven children in our family. But all seven of us went through
college. We did it because Papa gave us a little money and
a lot of inspiration.

CHARLES L. ALLEN

You made me so proud when you

You made me so embarrassed when you

The most precious things of life are near at hand.

JOHN BURROUGHS

Like many in the Midwest, Dad lived close to the soil. His hands were rough from a lifetime working the land. . . . Dad had fundamental values with few frills. . . . He was always looking for what was practical. There was no place for Dad like his own home. . . .

He would ask me, "How much do you love me?" and I would reply, "Bushels and bushels." Well, that was the largest measure I had ever seen my dad use when he carried feed to the pigs!

MARJORIE M. METZ
The Path Less Trod

Dad, there is one question
I have always wanted to ask you. _____

_____

_____

_____

_____

_____

One thing I have always wanted to tell you is

_____

_____

_____

_____

_____

_____

God's qualities are that he's tall with brown hair with a little
white in it, nice, caring, loves everybody, and is interesting—
kind of like my dad.

ELISABETH, 8

Take Time to Play Checkers

Tell me again of days gone by,

Help me recall the sounds and songs,

What matter if we can't return,

Back to the place where the heart belongs! . . .

In every memory there clings,

The sweetness of a faded flower!

And what the heart has loved the most,

Can never be mislaid or lost!

GRACE E. EASLEY

One of the most surprising things
you did when I was growing up was _____

_____

_____

_____

_____

_____

The funniest thing you ever did was _____

_____

_____

_____

_____

_____

He has achieved success who has lived well,

laughed often and loved much;

who has gained the respect of intelligent men

and the love of little children.

Mrs. A. J. Stanley

For many years my father was a general in the US Army.
He wasn't the typical image of an army general. He was a
"velvet-covered brick"—strong and decisive, but so warm
and gracious and encouraging in the process that he came
across as if his greatest pleasure was to help his subordinates
do their jobs well. Every command he had, officers asked to
serve under him.

ANNE ORTLUND
Disciplines of the Heart

Sometimes I think how my life would have been
different if you had not been my dad.

The things that impressed
me most about your job were _____

_____

_____

_____

_____

_____

These are some of the ways
your career influenced my life. _____

_____

_____

_____

_____

_____

One thing I like about my dad is he helps me with my
homework. . . . Another thing I like about him is his clothes
all match.

ERIKA, 9

Take Time to Play Checkers

I am so thankful for these moral values and principles you taught me.

1. _____

_____

2. _____

_____

3. _____

_____

4. _____

_____

When I think about what my daddy means to me, I am overwhelmed with joy and pride because he means the world to me. Because of his undying love for God, he is able to love his family unconditionally.

Every morning growing up at home, I always woke to my sweet daddy spending time reading God's Word, and throughout the day Jesus was definitely seen through him. I am so thankful for the godly example he has been for me and my precious family.

AMY BURT, 24

You are like no other dad. These are the unique characteristics that make you special.

_____

_____

_____

Some of your most endearing habits.

_____

_____

_____

Some of your craziest habits.

_____

_____

_____

_____

It is in loving—not in being loved—

The heart is blest;

It is in giving—not in seeking gifts—

We find our quest.

ANONYMOUS

The most important point in marriage is love and romance. People usually always like to have a little romance and tender love once in a while. It seems to make people feel really happy and warm inside.

MELISSA, 10

Take Time to Play Checkers

Some of the things I most appreciate
about your relationship with Mom are _____

_____

_____

_____

_____

_____

_____

This is what I have learned from you
about love and marriage. _____

_____

_____

_____

_____

_____

_____

Where there is great love there are always miracles.

WILLA CATHER

Lucky the child who can climb into that lap of safety and know, always, the confidence born of a father's love.

Victoria, JUNE 1995

When words failed us, my father and I had music. Through Bach, Brahms, and Schubert, we could express the deep feelings we were both too shy to acknowledge. The violin is his legacy to me. Like my father and his love, it is elegant and fragile—but surprisingly sturdy.

ELIZA THOMAS

Five reasons why I'm so glad you're my dad.

1. _____

_____

_____

2. _____

_____

_____

3. _____

_____

_____

4. _____

_____

_____

5. _____

_____

_____

Kind words are the music of the world.

FREDERICK WILLIAM FABER

I am still overwhelmed with those childhood feelings of anticipation as I pull into the driveway of my parents' home. . . . Mom is waiting to rush out the door with joyful hugs. It's hard though, because Dad isn't there. He's in heaven and, oh, how I miss him! So now when I go home, I'm overwhelmed with tears— tears of sadness and tears of gratefulness. My mind is flooded with flashbacks of all the times Dad was there to greet me. In my mind's eye, I can still see him clearly. I can almost feel his big arms around me, and I remember his steadfast love for me.

SUSAN ALEXANDER YATES
A House Full of Friends

A prayer for you, Dad, from your little girl.

Keep in mind that the essence of your prayers is the faith you have in them that they will be answered.

REBBE NACHMAN

Listen to me tell you that I love you. I like to hear you tell me that you love me.

CLAIR, 6

Take Time to Play Checkers

Photos

Photos

*L*ife is like an exciting
book, and every year
starts a new chapter.

ANONYMOUS

A Journal

Photos

Photos

Photos

Photos

My advice to any father is: "Don't forget your little girl. She may be growing up but she still loves sharing time with you."

BECKY, 15

Take Time to Play Checkers